Philip Ardagh's Shortcuts

A FAST AND FUNNY GUIDE TO

Marie Curie

Illustrated by Mike Phillips

MACMILLAN CHILDREN'S BOOKS

For my Polish pal,
'Val' Englert

First published 2000 by Macmillan Children's Books

This edition published 2013 by Macmillan Children's Books
an imprint of Pan Macmillan
20 New Wharf Road, London N1 9RR
Associated companies throughout the world
www.panmacmillan.com

ISBN 978-1-4472-4026-6

A CIP catalogue record for this book is available from the British Library.

Printed and bound by CPI Group (UK) Ltd, Croydon CR0 4YY

CONTENTS

USEFUL WORDS

Here are some useful words, some of which look very scientific but (if you're not a HUGE fan of science) don't panic. This book is also full of nice non-scientific words such as 'at', 'in', 'on' and 'the'.

Atoms The smallest part of an element that keeps the chemical properties of that element.

Chemical Properties The properties which make substances behave the way they do during a chemical reaction.

Chemical Reaction A process involving the change in the structure and energy of an atom but not its nucleus.

Chemistry A branch of science which deals with how substances are made up and how they act under different conditions.

Compound A combination of elements held together by a chemical reaction.

Doctorate The highest academic degree possible, in any area of knowledge.

Electrons Negatively charged subatomic particles.

Element A substance which can't be split into even simpler substances with a chemical reaction.

Isolate To separate something from everything else, so you have it in its pure form.

Nobel Prize Named after Alfred Nobel, inventor of dynamite, these annual awards, given by the Swedish Academy with money left in Nobel's will, are for physics, chemistry, medicine and physiology, literature, and world peace.

Nucleus A cluster of subatomic particles at the heart of an atom.

Physics A branch of science dealing with the properties of matter and energy and their relationship.

Pitchblende A soft, black rock containing uranium and radium.

Radioactive Giving off radiation.

Subatomic Any particle smaller than an atom.

Substance A material. Solids, powders and liquids are all examples of substances.

Thesis The written part of original research submitted by a candidate for a degree (in this case a doctorate).

WHEN MARIE WAS MARJA

Marie Curie was born Marja Sklodowska on 7 November 1867. She was Polish and born near the centre of the Polish capital, Warsaw. 'Marie' is the French version of her name which she used when she went to Paris. 'Curie' is the name she took when she later married a man by that name. To avoid confusion, I'll call her Marie from the start, or you might think I'm writing about two different people. It was as 'Marie Curie' that she became one of the most famous scientists – and certainly *the* most famous female scientist – the world has ever known.

A TROUBLED HOMELAND

Marie was born at a time when Poland was ruled by the Tsars of Russia (but not by more than one at once). The Poles had risen up against their foreign rulers on a number of occasions but had been crushed and defeated. Thousands and thousands of Poles were sent to work in chain gangs in Siberia (which was a bitterly cold place where many died). Marie's mother, Bronislawa, was the head teacher of a local school. Marie and her family lived with their parents in a flat in Freta Street, behind the school. She had three sisters – Zofia, Bronislawa (named after their mother – and later referred to as Bronia) and Helena – and a brother, Józef. In the Polish tradition, the girls' surname ended in an 'a', and Józef's ended in 'i', like his father's, to make Sklodowski. The Russian authority kept a beady eye on the establishment because it was run by Poles for Poles.

A THIRST FOR KNOWLEDGE

There's little doubt where Marie Curie got her love of science from: her father. Marie's father, Wladyslaw, had a number of jobs, including that of being an assistant director of a 'gymnasium' (which was an official Russian-run school). He was fascinated with science and liked to pass on what he knew to his children. Warsaw University had been closed by the Russians in the 1830s, but he'd continued to study there unofficially.

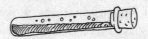

AN ODD UPBRINGING

Marie's father either made learning fun, or playing educational ... it depends on how you look at it! A game he used to play with the older children (Marie was the youngest) involved building everything from cities to mountains out of coloured building blocks around the flat! Every evening, they did keep fit exercises!

AN AMAZING MOTHER

Both of Marie's parents came from well-to-do backgrounds and her mother was a devout Roman Catholic. But neither of these things stopped Bronislawa from being a very independent and unusual woman. When the family moved from Freta Street to Nowolipki Street in 1868, Marie's mum decided to save money by making her children's shoes. She found that she was so good at it that she set up a cobbler's workshop below the flat! Many people would have thought this was a real let-down after having been a head teacher. Not Marie's mum! Sadly, when Marie was about four, her mother showed signs of having tuberculosis (sometimes called TB), a disease few people recovered from.

MONEY WORRIES

In 1873, the Sklodowski family had other worries. Marie's father was fired from his job as assistant director at the gymnasium (school) by the Russian authorities. The only way to make ends meet was for him to turn the flat into a small private boarding school, which was a bit of a squeeze! Children and students mixed, with about twenty people sitting down together at meal times. As well as live-in students, Marie's father took on extra pupils who just came for the lessons. The place was packed.

TRAGEDY AFTER TRAGEDY

The health of Marie's mother, Bronislawa, had worsened and, during this time, she went away from the over-crowded flat to Austria and France on 'rest cures'. It was hoped that the warmer climates might make her better. She was accompanied by her oldest daughter, Marie's sister Zofia (sometimes called Sophie in books). Tragically, it was Zofia who died next, not her mother. She caught typhus in 1874 and died on 31 January.

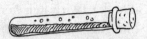

A MIGHTY KILLER

The typhus epidemic which swept Poland on a number of occasions had been brought to the country by the armies of Napoleon. Not on purpose, mind you. Typhus thrived in conditions where people were crowded and dirty – such as army camps – and the killer-organisms were passed from body to body by lice. Perhaps the crowded conditions of the boarding school brought the disease into Marie's flat.

FROM BAD TO WORSE

It was the TB, not typhus, that finally killed Marie's mother. She died on 9 May 1878, when Marie was ten years old. The day before, she summoned her remaining children to her bedside, and told them that she loved them all. The children had described their mother as 'the soul of the house' and there was a terrible feeling of loss. Marie became very depressed and would spend hours sitting in the corner crying.

MADAME JADWIGA SIKORSKA

Marie was now being taught at a private school run by Madame Jadwiga Sikorska. With her went Helena, a sister older by one year. The Russian authorities had very strict rules about what you could and could not teach, so teaching was on two levels: what the children were timetabled to learn (and would claim they were being taught if questioned) and what Madame Sikorska actually taught them as part of a good and proper Polish education.

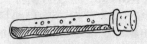

POLISH PRIDE

In the state-run gymnasia (which is what you call more than one gymnasium), children were forced to speak Russian rather than their native Polish. It was a matter of pride to many Poles, including Marie's family, to speak Polish as much as possible, doing their best to keep the language as pure and free from Russian influence as possible. (This is a little like the French who don't like English phrases such as 'le snack bar' sneaking into their language.) In 1878, the year of her mother's death, Marie was sent to Gymnasium Number Three.

UPS AND DOWNS

Marie seems to have had mixed views about her new school, where the teachers seemed to treat the pupils like enemies! Years later, she described how much she hated it. At the time, she told others how much she *liked* it there. However bad the teachers may have been, they can't have dampened her enthusiasm for finding out things. She had her own opinion on many topics and was happy to argue with the teachers about it! She graduated from the school in 1883, first in her class and with a gold medal.

NOT SO GOOD FOR GIRLS

Marie's brother Józef had already graduated first of his class and had also been given a gold medal and was now at the medical school of the (long since reopened) Warsaw University. The problem for his sister Marie was that girls weren't allowed into the university! This left Marie with three options: to get married, go to university abroad or to get a job.

THE FOURTH WAY

Suddenly, there was a fourth option. A woman called Jadwiga Szczasinska-Dawidowa (that's 26 letters long, if you were wondering) had set up a 'secret university' for women. This unofficial academy originally met at different flats to be taught by some of the top Polish scientists, historians and philosophers. More and more women joined, so the classes of what had now become known as the 'Flying University' – probably because it flew from place to place – were held in secret in some of the larger institutions. It was very important that the Russian authorities didn't find out. Marie became a student.

THE GOVERNESS

Marie needed to earn some money too, so she took a job as a governess and hated it. She didn't like the family she lived with and worked for and the relationship between them soon turned icy. In the end, she told the lady of the house just what she thought of her . . . and neither was sorry to see the back of the other! All the while, Marie was, of course, secretly studying at night.

MAKING PLANS

Marie and her sister Bronia came up with a scheme. Bronia would go off to university in Europe – after all, she was older than Marie – whilst Marie stayed behind, earning money to support her. Then, when Bronia had got her university degree and found a job, she would arrange for Marie to come over and it'd be Bronia's turn to support her. So off Bronia went to Paris . . . and Marie found herself another governess's position.

THE ZORAWSKIS

Now aged eighteen, Marie got a job with the Zorawski family in a place called Szczuki, fifty or so miles north of Warsaw. The house was slap-bang next to the family's sugar beet factory, so was probably a pretty noisy and smelly place to be. To begin with, she got on well with the children in her care, and their parents, and managed to read as many books as possible in what free time she had. It was during this time – she was with the Zorawskis for four years – that she realized that science interested her more than anything.

SCHOOL FOR PEASANTS

Not content with being a governess and doing her own studies, Marie set up unofficial classes for some of the local peasants. The Zorawskis were quite happy for Marie to do this. In fact, one of their daughters (called 'Bronka'), who was the same age as Marie, helped her out. This was a dangerous thing to do. If the Russian authorities found out that two Polish girls were holding these classes, Marie and Bronka could have found themselves in very serious trouble indeed.

ANOTHER KIND OF TROUBLE

It was something else that landed Marie in trouble with the Zorawski family, though. She fell in love with their son Kazimierz, a maths student at Warsaw University who was just a year older than her. They decided to get married, but his parents were having none of it. Yes, Marie was a good governess. Yes, they approved of the work she and Bronka did with the peasants. Yes, Marie was a highly intelligent young woman . . . but she was *poor*. They couldn't have their son marry a poor person! Marie felt betrayed, but had to carry on working in the house another year and three months! She finally left the Zorawski family in Easter 1889.

AT HOME AND ABROAD

Meanwhile, all was going well for Marie's sister Bronia in Paris. She was not only enjoying university life, but was also engaged to another Kazimierz! *Her* Kazimierz was one Kazimierz Dluskis. Back in Poland, Marie became governess to the Fuchs family at a fashionable resort on the Baltic coast. Although Marie recorded that Mr and Mrs Fuchs had terrible tempers, anyone seemed better than the Zorawskis!

'NO' TO PARIS

When the time came for Marie to put work behind her and to go to Paris as planned, she decided not to! She spent the next couple of years living with her father. Perhaps it was because she was still secretly seeing Kazimierz Zorawski. Perhaps she didn't like the idea of being too far away from her sister Helena and her beloved father. Whatever the reason, after all that, she decided to stay in Poland. For one thing, she could now work in a proper scientific laboratory. It was run by one of her cousins and some of the shh-oh-so-secret Flying University classes were held there. She also managed to do her own experiments in the lab in the evenings and at weekends.

ANOTHER CHANGE OF PLAN

In summer 1891, Marie went to the Tatra Mountains. There were two main reasons for the trip. Firstly, she wasn't well. Her mother had died and her sister had died, so matters of health were taken very seriously in her family. The mountain air might do her good. Secondly, she needed to have a serious think. Bronia had sent her another invitation to Paris . . . so should she stay and try and make a life for herself in Poland, or take the plunge and finally go to Paris? She decided to go.

Marie in Paris
(This Rhymes in French)

Marie arrived in France in November 1891. To begin with, she lived in her sister Bronia and husband Kazimierz Dluskis's home. Marie did not get much peace and quiet. Dluskis was a political activist, and the house was always packed with people. Six months after starting at the science faculty in the Sorbonne (the University of Paris), she moved into a tiny flat of her own.

THE DLUSKISES

Later, Bronia and her husband set up a modern tuberculosis sanatorium in the Carpathian Mountains. Marie's sister wanted to do something to help others who suffered from the disease that had killed their mother. Bronia and Kazimierz travelled widely, whipping up support and funds for the Zakopane Sanatorium, which finally got under construction in 1899.

ALONE IN A CROWD

After years of living with her brother and sisters, then with students and later with families (when she was a governess), Marie was now living alone for the first time. She had a cheap flat on a top floor, which was very cold in winter but ideal for studying uninterrupted. But a woman student studying at the Sorbonne was alone in another way too . . . such students were few and far between. There was no way Marie could blend into the background. For some reason, it was more acceptable for 'foreign' women to go to university – perhaps they didn't know better! – but the few French women who went had the toughest time. Of the 1,820 plus students in the science faculty, Marie was one of only 23 women.

A STAR PERFORMANCE

To say that Marie was an excellent student would be a bit like saying that the sun is quite hot, or that Julius Caesar was quite a well-known Roman ruler. She was brilliant. She not only got the highest marks in the *licence ès science* exams in 1892, she went on to get the second highest marks in the *licence ès mathématiques* (you guessed it, maths) in

1894 . . . and she was 'only' a woman. That showed 'em! (A licence is what we call a degree.)

PIERRE'S HERE!

It was in spring 1894 that Marie was introduced to a man named Pierre Curie by a Pole called Joseph Kowalski. Now, even if I hadn't mentioned on page 8 that she married a man named Curie, you might have guessed it. The clue is in the name she's best known by (Marie C-U-R-I-E, when she started out as a Sklodowska). When they met, however, neither had love on their mind. Marie was still getting over breaking up with Kazimierz Zorawski, and Pierre had never got over the death of his childhood sweetheart. Anyway, the reason for the meeting was to discuss the practical problem of finding lab space!

A VERY MODEST MAN

Pierre Curie was a very talented scientist. By the time he met Marie, when he was thirty-five, he'd made a number of important discoveries about magnetism and about crystals and had also designed some useful pieces of scientific equipment. Because he didn't teach at one of the famous universities, though, he wasn't well-known. When a director of the industrial physics and chemistry institution where he worked wanted to put Pierre's name forward for a scientific award, Pierre urged him not to.

PIERRE'S PAST

Pierre was born in Paris on 15 May 1859 (which means that he was eight-and-a-half years older than Marie). His mother's brothers were inventors. His father was a doctor. Pierre's father taught him and his big brother Jacques at home. Unusually for the time, no religion was taught or practised in the Curie household. Then, when Pierre was fourteen, a tutor named Albert Bazille was employed . . . two years later, the sixteen-year-old had passed the *bachelier ès sciences* which got him a place at the Sorbonne. Two years after that, he graduated with his *licence ès sciences* and was instantly offered a job as a lab assistant in the physics department. His brother Jacques held the same position in the mineralogy labs. The two worked together, publishing nine scientific papers about crystals.

A FRIENDSHIP BLOSSOMS

It was clear from the start that Marie and Pierre had a lot in common. They were both brilliant, hardworking scientists from unusual backgrounds. In a way, they were both 'outsiders', not easily fitting into the French scientific establishment. One of Pierre's first gifts to Marie was a copy of one of his scientific papers! Far better than a bunch of flowers or a box of chocolates. He wanted to marry her.

She, on the other hand, was going back to Poland for a holiday, before deciding what to do.

ON THE UP AND UP

Although apart, Marie and Pierre kept in touch by letter and the matter of marriage was raised. After years of not bothering, Pierre then wrote up a thesis and applied for a doctorate at the Sorbonne. It's likely that he did this to please Marie, who was proud of his achievements. He was awarded his doctorate and he and his brother also received some science prizes for their discoveries about crystals. Not only that, Pierre was made a professor at the *École de physique et chimie*. In summer 1895, Marie returned to Paris and their engagement was announced.

MEET MARIE CURIE

Marie and Pierre married on 26 July 1895 at the Town Hall in Sceaux, on the outskirts of Paris, not far from Pierre's parents' house where the reception was held afterwards. As well as Marie's sister Bronia and husband Kazimierz, who'd come from Paris, her father and sister Helena came over from Warsaw. After the wedding, Marie and Pierre went off on honeymoon: a cycling holiday in Brittany.

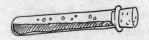

PEDAL POWER

Bicycles were all the rage in Europe in the 1890s. One of the most significant things about them was that they were very difficult to ride in a skirt – so special cycling clothes had to be designed for women cyclists: culottes, or 'blousy knickers'. Women often also wore straw boaters (a kind of hat usually worn by men). Some historians argue that bicycles did more to lead to the relaxing of what women 'should' and 'should not' wear, and to the emancipation of women than years of fighting for rights! (Because Marie kept notebooks detailing all her expenses over the years, we know she spent a lot on her beloved bike.)

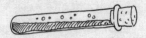

HOME SWEET HOME

Marie and Pierre set up home in a three room flat on the *rue de la Glacière* (which means 'road of the glacier', though there wasn't a glacier in sight). On 12 September 1897, their first child, a daughter called Irène, was born. A few weeks later, Pierre's mother died and, soon after that, Pierre's father moved in with them.

THE NOTEBOOKS OF MARIE CURIE

A very useful source of information for anyone wanting to find out about the life of Marie Curie is her notebooks. She kept notebooks on her experiments. She kept notebooks on her children. She kept notebooks on how much she spent on absolutely everything. Sometimes she would write recipes in the margins next to experiments, draw doodles or simply make a note of something which tickled her fancy. They're jam-packed full of everything. Sadly, today, some of these notebooks are radioactive and would be dangerous to leaf through without protection.

THE REAL WORK BEGINS

Now Marie Curie decided to turn her attention to important scientific matters. In March 1896 Henri Becquerel, a well-known physicist at the Natural History Museum in Paris, had noted a strange phenomenon. He had noticed that compounds which contained an element called uranium gave off 'rays of a peculiar character' a bit like X-rays. What he hadn't done was found out what these rays were and why they were given off. And that was what Marie found so intriguing.

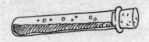

X-RAYS

X-rays were discovered by the German physicist Wilhelm Conrad Roentgen in 1895 . . . by mistake. He was actually studying something called cathode rays but discovered these invisible rays that could pass through black cardboard and light up a phosphorescent screen the other side. He called them 'X-rays' because X is the letter scientists give to an unknown quantity (like in The X-Files™). He soon found that he could take X-ray pictures of the insides of objects, including the bones that made up his wife's hand. X-rays caught the imagination of the public world-wide and were believed to have amazing healing powers. Roentgen did not patent any of his discoveries (so that X-rays could be used by everyone) and died penniless.

BECQUEREL INVESTIGATES

Becquerel's discovery of uranium compounds giving off rays was an accident too. He was experimenting with uranium salts, sprinkled on top of black card wrapped around photographic plates. He believed that if an object (such as a coin or key) was placed on the salts and left in the sunlight long enough, it would – after a number of hours – leave an impression of the object on the photographic plate. (The salts were a substitute for the phosphorescent screen in Roentgen's experiments.)

One day, Becquerel had a metal cross set up in such a way but, being a grey day, there was no sunlight so he was about to give up. To his amazement, he found that, light or no light, something had caused the cross to leave an impression on the photographic plate. The uranium salts must themselves be giving off invisible rays! He tried many other substances after that, but the experiment only worked with uranium. What Becquerel had discovered was what we know as radioactivity. The only trouble was, he didn't know it!

THE CURIES STEP IN

Whilst everyone else, scientists and public alike, seemed to be getting all excited over X-rays, Marie decided that Becquerel's discovery was well worth further investigation. Not only did it seem most intriguing but the field was clear – no one else seemed the slightest bit interested in it (including Becquerel himself, who thought he'd discovered all that there was to discover about uranium). So, in winter 1897, Marie began her work on uranium.

LET THE EXPERIMENTS COMMENCE

Now, dear *GET A LIFE!* reader, this is a book about the life of Marie Curie, not a science text book explaining exactly what experiments she set up, how she carried them out and what the results were. I'm sure there's a place for books like that – probably on a shelf marked 'FOR BRAINY SCIENTIST-TYPE PEOPLE ONLY', but there's no place for it in the fast, fun and (though I say it myself) fantabulous *GET A LIFE!* series . . . so there. You have been warned. If you were hoping to use this as a guide to your own highly dangerous experiments with uranium; tough luck. If you were worried things were about to get far toooooooooo complicated; relax.

NOT MUCH OF A LAB

Marie had been used to working in what were then considered the 'state of the art', 'up to the minute' laboratories at the Sorbonne. Now she was working in an old storeroom of the school where Pierre was teaching. But, although she had to use rickety old tables for work benches and made equipment from old crates, she didn't have to answer to anyone else but herself. In this lab she was in charge.

THE FIRST TESTS

Marie started off by checking the claim made by Becquerel (and a well-known British scientist called Lord Kelvin) that uranium rays could make the air conduct electricity. Normally, a metal plate charged by a battery can only charge another metal plate if the two are touching or connected by, say, a wire. By putting uranium on a charged metal plate, Marie Curie wanted to see if the air around it would become charged, act like a wire and charge the second plate. It did. She could also tell whether a particular source of uranium (or other substance) gave off more or less energy than another by the speed with which the second plate was charged and by how much.

ON THE SCROUNGE

Being a proper scientist, Marie didn't stick to uranium simply because it was uranium she was investigating. She wanted to compare uranium with other substances, to help her try to fathom out why it was so special. She tried element after element, compound after compound but none of them caused the second plate to charge up with electricity. Then, on 17 February 1898, she tried with a compound known as pitchblende. It produced much more energy and a much stronger current than uranium ever had!

HAVE YOU SEEN MY OTHER SLIPPER, MY SWEET?

I'M JUST RUNNING A FEW TESTS ON IT

PITCHBLENDE AND URANIUM

Uranium, named after the planet Uranus, was discovered in 1789 by an amateur chemist named Martin Heinrich Klaproth. He found it in a mineral compound called pitchblende. While the metallic element uranium aroused much interest, pitchblende was mainly seen as a useful source of the element, rather than of being any interest or use on its own. Being a compound, pitchblende is created as a result of a chemical reaction between the elements which make it up. In other words, it's not simply a mixture of different elements which can easily be sorted out (like different coloured marbles). You – or, in this case Marie and Pierre – would need to use chemistry to separate the different elements.

SURPRISE, SURPRISE

Once again, Marie tested other uranium compounds and pure uranium and then the pitchblende. The pure uranium gave off more energy (was more 'active') than the compounds . . . except for the pitchblende which was the most active of all. But what to do next? Marie reasoned that if pitchblende had been such a surprise, what else might be out there? She now tested just about anything she could lay her hands on and, low and behold, she found that a mineral called aeschynite was also more active than uranium. Unlike pitchblende, however, the aeschynite didn't even contain uranium. What was going on?

PUTTING IT TOGETHER

Aeschynite contains an element called thorium, so Marie – with the aid of husband Pierre – now set about checking the scientific properties of all compounds containing uranium and thorium. Marie believed that, as well as uranium, pitchblende must contain another element which gave off even more power than the uranium. In other words, it must be even more active.

THE MIGHT OF CALCITE

Marie and Pierre discovered that yet another mineral, called calcite, was also highly active. The good thing about calcite was that an artificial form was easy enough to create in the lab. Natural calcite gave off a high energy reading. Lab-created calcite didn't, so this suggested that natural calcite contained an unknown element more powerful than uranium, as did pitchblende.

REPORT TO THE ACADEMY

The French Academy of Sciences – which I'll be calling the Academy, from now on – was given a work-in-progress report on Marie and Pierre's behalf by one of Marie's old teachers, Gabriel Lippman. (The Curies couldn't deliver it because neither of them was a member.) With hindsight, the information this report contained was pretty mind-blowing. Not only had it suggested that there was a new element waiting to be discovered in pitchblende and natural calcite, but also that Marie Curie had used 'activity' (what we now think of as radioactivity) to suggest it existed. This was ground-breaking stuff!

THE ELUSIVE POLONIUM

Meanwhile, the work went on. Marie and Pierre did all they could to try to isolate this element more active than uranium. With the help of a chemist called Gustave

Bémont, they managed to further separate elements of pitchblende and were left with samples 150 times, 300 times, 330 times and 400 times more active than uranium – but couldn't extract the single new element on its own. But they were now confident enough that there was a new element in there to give it a name. They called it polonium after Poland, Marie's country of birth. In the paper that announced this, they also used the word *radioactive* – okay, so they spelled it 'radio-active' with a hyphen and in French, but it's the same thing. They had invented a new term that was soon used the world over.

RADIUM

After the discovery of polonium, the discovery of yet *another* new element soon followed. In November and December of 1898 – again with the help of Gustave Bémont – the Curies worked on extracting an element from a compound containing barium (taken from pitchblende) which was 900 times more radioactive than uranium. Yup, you read that right: 900 times! They called it radium, after the Latin word *radius* meaning 'ray'. They sent a report of their findings to the Academy.

SURPRISE PRIZE

Research cost money and the Academy had already given Marie Curie 3,800 French francs as a prize for her work. It was very unusual (if not unique) to award a prize to a WOMAN – shock! horror! – so they kept pretty quiet about it, telling Pierre and getting him to tell his wife! Marie and Pierre received a fair amount of money in the form of prizes over the years. They also received help from Becquerel (who'd first observed the rays given off by uranium and whose influence they acknowledged) but, for some reason, the Curies never seemed to fully trust the man himself.

THE RACE FOR RADIUM

Although the Curies had confirmed the existence of the element radium within the 'active' barium compound – with the help of a scientist called Eugène Demarçay who had a machine called a spectrograph – they hadn't actually been able to isolate the element so as to have a piece of radium and nothing but radium. This was now to be Marie's task. It would be the only way to provide 100 per cent proof of its existence. Pierre, meanwhile, would try to work out what this 'radioactivity' that they'd discovered was all about!

THE BIRTH OF THE ATOM

Back in 1807, a chap called Dalton had presented his Atomic Theory. In it, he said that all matter is made up of tiny particles called atoms, that atoms of the same element are alike, that chemical reactions are really atoms rearranging themselves, and that atoms can't be made, destroyed or divided. In the late 1890s, when Marie and Pierre were hard at work on radioactivity, British scientist J. J. Thompson was working on his 'plum pudding' model of the atom. It showed it containing negatively charged grains – which he called cathode rays but were later called electrons. At the turn of the century, the physicist Ernest Rutherford came up with a model showing the electrons circling a positively charged nucleus. These were the very early days of nuclear physics that would eventually lead to the atom bomb and beyond.

MAKING A MOVE

Marie desperately needed a bigger laboratory, so the Curies moved across the courtyard to what had once been a dissection room (where dead bodies were cut up by medical students). It was really nothing more than a giant shed! The roof was made of glass so was hot in summer, but leaked terribly in the wet. There was a stove to keep her warm, but it never worked properly.

SEE! THE NEW LAB EVEN HAS RUNNING WATER!

HARD GRAFT

It was only thanks to donations from the Academy and from generous benefactors that Marie was able to carry out her work. She didn't have a paid university post or any official funding. She needed over ten tonnes of pitchblende for starters! It was cheaper to buy it with the (expensive) uranium already removed, and was even more suited for her purposes that way anyway. It arrived in her giant, leaky shed by the sack-load. Marie didn't only need brains and determination in her work, but strength too. She spent much of her time heaving materials around, stirring great vats of liquid and building up her muscles!

DEATH GLOW

One of the discoveries that Marie Curie made was that the metals – she called them 'new metals' – that contained radium were luminous. In other words, they glowed. Marie was delighted. Sometimes she would line them up and look at the light they gave off. There was something almost magical about the glow. Tragically, what no one knew then was how harmful radioactive substances were. These 'pretty' rays were killers.

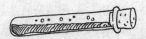

ALPHA AND BETA RAYS

At the beginning of 1899, the physicist Ernest Rutherford (already mentioned on page 35) published the results of his research which suggested that radioactive substances gave off two types of rays: alpha rays and beta rays. Alpha and beta are the names of the first two letters of the Greek alphabet . . . Not that Rutherford was

Greek. He wasn't. He was born in New Zealand. Alpha rays were much stronger than beta rays, but couldn't pass through barriers. The 'weaker' beta rays passed through thick barriers, no sweat.

THE BIGGER PICTURE

Marie, Pierre and Becquerel looked at Ernest Rutherford's findings and, by the end of the year had concluded that what Rutherford called beta rays were, in fact, exactly the same as J. J. Thompson's cathode rays (now called electrons). These were the negatively charged particles in his plum pudding model. Little by little, the Curies were beginning to build up a picture of what they were dealing with.

THE LATEST REPORT

In 1900, there was a huge fair held in Paris to celebrate art and technology. Called the Universal Exposition, it attracted just under fifty million visitors. To mark the event, the International Congress of Physics was held, attracting some of the biggest names in science from all over the world. Here, Marie and Pierre presented a report on all their findings, and radioactivity became *the* talking point of the congress.

NO GO

1900 was also the year that Marie and Pierre were offered a real change of fortunes. The University of Geneva in Switzerland offered Pierre a chair. This wasn't a piece of furniture, but an important university post. If the Curies accepted, they'd have a specially equipped laboratory, two assistants to help them and would both have a salary . . . even though Marie's job title was left rather unclear. This seemed like far too good an opportunity to miss. They accepted. Then, while on holiday that summer, the Curies changed their minds. Why? Who knows. Whatever the reason, they decided to stay in their large, leaky shed. At least there they could be sure of total control.

OTHER MOVES

One move which did take place that year was from the Curie's flat in the *rue de la Glacière* to a house on the *boulevard Kellerman*. Marie, Pierre and Pierre's father's new home was on the quieter outskirts of Paris. Both Marie and Pierre also moved into new jobs to help pay for their experiments. Marie got a job at a well-respected school for women teachers (she'd trained as a teacher when she'd first married) and Pierre was given a number of new posts. It wasn't the jobs themselves that mattered to Marie and Pierre. It was the money they'd bring in to help them continue with their experiments.

AMAZING NEIGHBOURS

New neighbours, called the Perrins, were to move in next to the Curies in their new home. Amazingly, Mr Perrin came up with the stunningly advanced idea, in 1901, that an atom was really like a tiny solar system with its subatomic particles behaving like planets orbiting the sun. Not only that, in 1926, he went on to win a Nobel Prize. (And, if you don't know what they are, fear not. There'll be plenty more about them later on.)

THE RADIATION SPREADS

In 1901, Marie realized that just about everything in her leaky lab had become radioactive. At first, she'd suspected that it might have been because there was radioactive dust all over the place (a bit like finding sand in your socks a week after coming home from the beach), but then she blamed it on 'radioactive gas'. She believed that the glowing radioactive substances must create a gas in the air which then spread the radioactivity.

A PUZZLING PROBLEM

Something which greatly puzzled Pierre Curie was something he'd discovered quite by chance. When preparing to experiment with a piece of pure uranium – the element, not a compound; it was supposed to be uranium and nothing else – he actually managed to separate the radioactivity from the uranium. He had somehow extracted a new and highly radioactive substance from uranium . . . but how could that be possible? The new substance must be another type of uranium, he reasoned. It was still uranium, but a different variation. He called it uranium X. (As with X-rays, the X denoted the unknown.) The Curies realized that, when dealing with radioactive elements, the elements didn't seem to behave like ordinary elements. They followed different rules. Radioactive elements were *unstable*.

A COUPLE OF POSSIBILITIES

The Curies decided that there were two real possibilities about why radioactive substances behaved the way they did. One was that the atom of a radioactive element contained potential energy – energy just waiting to be released. In other words, the energy is already in there, waiting to do something. The other possibility was that these atoms got their energy – their radioactivity – from somewhere else. That makes sense, of course, because if an atom doesn't already have the energy, it has to get it from somewhere else. But which was the truth?

THE SUBATOMIC LEVEL

Rutherford and others now put the next piece of this scientific jigsaw into place. They decided that radioactivity was happening as a result of what they called 'subatomic chemical change'. In other words, for elements to be radioactive, chemical changes had to be taking place amongst the even smaller particles that make up atoms. Radioactivity, he decided, was a release of these subatomic particles. Scientists were used to dealing with most types of chemical reactions, could they ever hope to control chemical changes at *subatomic* level? It seemed unlikely.

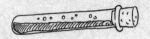

SUCCESS!

Neither Marie nor Pierre Curie were convinced by Rutherford's ideas and, anyway, Marie was far too busy still trying to isolate radium to give it *toooo* much thought. Finally, in July 1902, Marie was successful. After devoting three – almost four – years of her life to the task, she managed to extract a tiny, tiny, tiny amount of pure radium. This was the first time anyone had ever seen a pure piece of radium on its own. Now no one could dispute its existence. This was a fantastic achievement though, at about that time, Marie herself was beginning to doubt the existence of the other element they thought they'd discovered. She now believed that it was possible (if not likely) that polonium might be nothing more than a variation of another radioactive compound.

THE DEATH OF A FATHER

When Marie's father, Wladyslaw, learnt of his daughter's success, he described radium as 'the most costly of elements'. It had taken up so much of his daughter's time to isolate such a small amount. As it was, Wladyslaw's own time was running out. He had gallstones and needed an emergency operation to remove them. He died on 14 May 1902, aged 70. The funeral was delayed to allow Marie time to get there, and the coffin opened especially so that she could have one last look at his face.

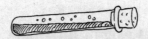

WILLY ON THE CASE

Scientists were excited at the prospect of discovering new elements and one in Germany, named Willy Marckward, thought he'd found one. He called it radiotellurium. Marie strongly suspected that it was really her polonium under a different name!

It didn't have exactly the same properties that's true, but that's because of the very nature of a radioactive substance. It'll give off different readings from one day to the next. Soon, Rutherford and others agreed that, more likely than not, Willy Marckward's radiotellurium was Marie's polonium. In 1906, Marie was able to prove that she was right.

A PAIR OF OUTSIDERS

Marie was often overlooked because she was a woman. Some scientists often referred to just one Curie, as though Pierre did all the work. But Pierre too suffered from being a scientist who wanted to do things his own way. Twice, he failed to get a chair at the Sorbonne. (I've done the furniture gag already, so you know what I mean.) He was put forward for the membership of the Academy but wasn't elected. Having said that, he didn't do himself any favours. When he was offered France's highest award, the Legion of Honour, he simply turned it down. He didn't believe in honours!

WHAT'S UP DOC?

Marie didn't actually become a Doctor of Physics until after she'd isolated radium. The reason why was simple: she'd been too busy working to finish her thesis. With the existence of radium now proven, she found time and the thesis was submitted. She was awarded her doctorate with the mention *très honorable* which, even with my bad French, I know means 'very honourable'. This was hardly surprising. She'd already made some major breakthroughs in scientific study! On the same day she was awarded her doctorate, Rutherford stopped off at the house of a scientist named Paul Langevin. Langevin invited the Curies around, so they finally got to meet Rutherford face-to-face.

FAILING HEALTH

People were beginning to notice that neither Marie nor Pierre were looking too good. They looked baggy-eyed and tired. Unfortunately, the Curies assumed it was because they'd been working all hours, snatching food and sleep when they could. Little did they know – and how could they? – that their ill health had a lot more to do with being exposed to massive amounts of radiation than with late nights. Sometimes, the skin came off their hands! In 1903, Marie spent much of the summer, on and off, in bed.

RECOGNITION AT LAST

In 1902, Pierre Curie's name was put forward for a Nobel Prize, the highest award a scientist could ever hope to achieve. Yup. Just Pierre's. No, that's not strictly true. It was suggested that the prize be shared between him and someone else who'd played a key part in the study of radioactivity: Henri Becquerel. (If you haven't fallen off your chair in shock, that's probably because you weren't sitting down to start with.) Marie didn't even get a mention. The reason? Yes, it was because she was a woman.

THE TRUTH COMES OUT

Fortunately, Marie had some allies. Of course, when Pierre learnt of the snub, he was horrified and wrote suggesting (in the politest of terms) that it would be rather nice if they'd consider his wife for the prize too. But he had no say in the matter. A mathematician called Gustav Mittag-Leffler, however, did. He was a member of the Swedish Academy of Sciences, which awarded the prizes, and was a supporter of women scientists. Eventually, her name appeared on a nomination along with Pierre's and Becquerel's.

ANOTHER FIRST

So Marie Curie became the first woman to receive a Nobel Prize. It would be another eight years before a woman scientist won a Nobel Prize again . . . and that was to be her too! The next woman scientist Nobel Prize winner after that was Marie and Pierre's own daughter, Irène, in 1935! Marie and Pierre didn't go to Sweden to collect their prize (of gold medal, diploma and cash) because of Marie's ill health. Of course, Pierre could have gone on his own, but he was never one for ceremonies. Not only that, he had no idea that it was the King of Sweden himself who was handing out the prizes nor that the cash part of it was HUGE. To be fair, being only the third year Nobel Prizes were being given out, the awards weren't as well-known as they are today.

A GOOD STORY

Marie Curie's scientific discoveries alone made a good story for the newspapers. The fact that she was a woman made it even more of a novelty. Winning the prize brought much publicity to the Curies and also many – often unwelcome – visits from reporters. Marie and Pierre wanted to get on with their work uninterrupted and didn't enjoy being celebrities, but the money came in handy. The Curies gave a large amount to Marie's sister Bronia and her husband Kazimierz for the Zakopane Sanitorium, but her sister Helena and Pierre's brother Jacques benefited too.

OTHER CHANGES

At long last, Pierre was made a member of the Academy. It was hardly surprising . . . he was now one of the most famous scientists in the world. When he was, for a second time, offered the Legion of Honour, he pointed out that he had no need of a decoration but great need for a decent laboratory! In December 1903, a new chair was created for 'general physics' at the Sorbonne, especially for Pierre.

ANOTHER CURIE

Just under two years later, on 6 December 1904, Marie and Pierre's second child, Eve, was born. Now Marie had to add babycare to all her lists of duties from working in the lab and writing papers to teaching, and giving talks and interviews. In the spring, they'd finally gone to Sweden to officially accept their share of the Nobel Prize. Pierre gave the speech for the both of them, but made sure that he mentioned Marie plenty of times.

DISASTER LOOMS

As time went on, Pierre complained more and more about aches and pains and Marie became seriously worried about his health. Tragically, Pierre was to die in April 1906, but not as a result of radiation poisoning. He was killed in an accident. Whilst Marie was staying in the country, Pierre was back in Paris, attending various meetings. On 19 April, a wet Thursday, he met with a number of colleagues including Joseph Kowalski, the man who'd first introduced him to Marie (way back on page 21). Later, he and his next-door neighbour Jean Perrin headed off together, then split up. Pierre headed off to see his publisher, while Perrin went off to a library. It was pouring with rain.

UNDER THE WHEELS

Hurrying across the road, Pierre was knocked down and killed instantly by a huge, heavy cart pulled by two horses. Angry onlookers tried to attack the poor driver, Louis Manin, who had to be protected by policemen running to the scene. An inquiry later decided that the accident came about for a variety of reasons: bad weather, poor visibility – it had been difficult for anyone to see clearly in the pouring rain – and, most importantly, the fact that Pierre hadn't been paying full attention. As was so often the case, his mind was probably more on scientific matters than on what was going on around him.

WORLD NEWS

The news of Pierre's death hit the headlines around the world, but it hit poor Marie the hardest. She had imagined working in the laboratory with Pierre at her side for many, many years to come. It seemed a lonely empty place without him. The scientific work would have to continue, but alone.

LIFE AFTER PIERRE

Pierre Curie was buried in Sceaux, the town where he and Marie had got married. In his coffin were a bunch of flowers and a photo of Marie. Instead of the coffin being draped in traditional black, Marie had it covered with bright and colourful flowers for the funeral procession. Although Marie wanted a small ceremony, many people came to the cemetery to pay their last respects. Her brother Józef and sister Bronia were there to give her support, along with Pierre's brother Jacques.

AN EMPTY CHAIR

With Pierre dead, the position that had been especially created for him at the Sorbonne was now empty. It would, of course, have made perfect sense simply to give the job to Marie. But sense didn't come into it. Marie was a WOMAN. Instead, they offered her exactly the same job that her husband'd had, but with the less important title of the director of the laboratory. In other words, she'd be performing exactly the same duties but without the prestige or importance. In May 1906, she accepted.

A STANDING OVATION

In November, Marie Curie became the first woman in the university's history to teach at the Sorbonne. The lecture theatre was packed and when she walked in, members of the audience leapt to their feet and clapped. Hundreds had gathered at the gate the day before, to be sure of a place. Even though she'd been to visit his grave the day before, she made no mention of Pierre. Instead, she launched straight into her lecture. She was an instant hit.

TO SCEAUX

In 1907, Marie left the *boulevard Kellerman* on the outskirts of Paris and moved, with Pierre's father and her daughters Irène and Eve, to a house in the *rue Chemin de fer* in Sceaux. She didn't particularly like her new house, but she was near the cemetery where Pierre was buried and that was what mattered.

A SCHOOLING OF SORTS

After Pierre's death, Marie set up a kind of 'schooling co-operative' where children of a group of friends got together and were taught different subjects by different parents. (These included Marie's old next-door neighbour and friends, the Perrins.) There was no school building, so the children would meet at different times in different houses. It must have reminded Marie of the students in her own house as a child and probably of the secret Flying University back in Poland. When Marie was at work in the lab, her father-in-law and a Polish governess (there were a number of different ones over the years) looked after Irène and Eve. Over time, it became obvious that Irène was very brainy and that Eve had a great musical talent.

TROUBLE AT THE LANGEVINS'

Paul Langevin – who had introduced the Curies to the British scientist Rutherford – was part of the school co-operative, along with his wife and children. His marriage was a rocky one, which is a polite way of saying that he and his wife had lots of arguments. She used to steal his letters and keep them as 'evidence' against him, and he used to hide money at work so she couldn't spend it! Once, in a flaming row, Paul was hit with an iron chair. He told his colleague that he'd fallen off his bike. Another time, he claimed that she'd hit him over the head with a bottle!

PIERRE'S FATHER DIES

In February 1910, Irène and Eve's grandfather died. He had been the centre of Curie family life and they all missed him terribly. So that he could be buried *under* his son's coffin, Pierre's coffin had to be dug up, taken out and put back on top after his father's had been lowered into the hole!

OUT OF HONOUR TO PIERRE

In that same year, Marie was offered the Legion of Honour – as Pierre had been twice before – and, like Pierre she turned it down. It wasn't that Marie was against public recognition and honours; far from it. She simply felt that it would be wrong for her to accept what Pierre had always declined.

A FRIEND INDEED

Paul Langevin had been a friend of both Pierre and Marie. Their paths had crossed many times. Langevin had been taught *by* Pierre and taught *with* Marie. He'd also been taught by J. J. Thompson and, having a sharp mind, became an excellent scientist. He was very upset by Pierre's death and paid him a fine public tribute. Then, with Pierre gone and his own marriage a complete mess, Langevin and Marie became more than just friends. They fell in love. (*Now* you can see why he's so important in this book.)

REVENGE!

It didn't take Paul Langevin's wife Jeanne long to suspect that Marie and her husband were up to something. Soon she had proof. Her letter-pinching skills came into play once more and she managed to get hold of a letter Langevin had planned to send to Marie. Jeanne told Jean Perrin that she intended to send it to the newspapers to ruin Marie's reputation. Perrin begged her not to. Next, Jeanne confronted Marie in the street. She shouted abuse at her and told her to get out of France! Later, she threatened to kill Marie if she didn't go.

WHY DO I GET THE FEELING YOU DON'T LIKE ME ?

AGREEMENT IS REACHED

Good old Perrin managed to negotiate a peace between the warring parties. If Langevin and Marie promised to stop seeing anything of each other, even for work, Jeanne wouldn't go to the papers or kill Marie for not leaving France!

YET MORE HONOURS

That September, Marie attended the International Congress of Radiology and Electricity in Brussels, Belgium. Here it was agreed that there should be an 'international standard for radium' against which all radium samples would be expressed. In other words, they needed one piece of radium against which to judge and measure all others. It was agreed that Marie should prepare this radium. Not only that, it was agreed that – in the same way time is measured in units of seconds – the unit of radium would be measured in 'curies', in honour of Pierre.

A PLACE IN THE ACADEMY?

That autumn, a place came up for grabs at the Academy. As a Nobel Prize winner, Marie seemed the obvious choice and a number of friends and colleagues urged her to put her name forward for it, woman or not. It wasn't only men who were against the idea of a woman member, though, some women were too. On 24 January 1911, it was put to the all-male members. Marie lost by two votes.

OUTRAGE!

Marie's supporters were outraged. On a purely scientific level, Marie had been streets ahead of the other candidates. That was obvious. As well as all the work she'd done before Pierre's death, she'd gone on to conduct other experiments to check theories on radioactivity put forward by other scientists. After years of hard work, she had more radium than other scientists, so could carry out experiments that they could only dream of. When it came to information about radioactivity and radiation, Marie Curie had become the most reliable source on the planet! Having 'dared' to put her name forward for the Academy, however, she'd now made herself a lot of new enemies too.

DROPPING A BOMBSHELL

As if things weren't bad enough, Jeanne Langevin apparently arranged a spot more letter-pinching (even though she didn't actually do it herself this time) and discovered that Marie and her husband had, indeed, been keeping in touch. Unfortunately for Marie, these letters ended up in the hands of one Henri Bourgeois. As well as being Jeanne's brother-in-law, Bourgeois was also the editor of a newspaper, and he went to see Marie. She took Perrin's advice to leave Paris for a while.

LANGEVIN LEAVES

In July 1911, Langevin and his wife Jeanne split up. After another row (where she claimed he hit her) Langevin got out of the house taking two of their sons with him. Langevin claimed that he was just taking them on holiday. Jeanne claimed that he'd walked out on her. Either way, she filed for divorce. Not long after that, Langevin and Marie's love affair became public. The French newspapers lapped it up. What a scandal! Most of the stories were told from 'poor' Jeanne's point of view with her husband and Marie (in particular) made out to be the villains.

ANOTHER FIRST

In the middle of all this scandal, when doubts were beginning to be cast on some of the newspapers' versions of events, it was announced that Marie Curie had been awarded her second Nobel Prize. She was the first person, let alone woman, to have won TWO Nobel Prizes. This time it was for chemistry and her work on radium. When she'd won her first prize, the French press had been wild with excitement. This time, the news barely got a mention. Fortunately, scientists such as Albert Einstein were on her side.

A CAUSE FOR EMBARRASSMENT

The Swedish Academy which gave out the Nobel Prizes was deeply embarrassed by the scandal surrounding Marie's love for Langevin. In November 1911, they even suggested that she shouldn't come to the award ceremony. Marie's response was blunt. In a written reply, she stated that, as far as she could see, there was no connection between her scientific and private lives and that she would, indeed, be going to Sweden . . . and she did, with her sister Bronia and daughter Irène. But she was far from well. Returning to France, she was rushed to hospital. When she came out, her health remained poor for the rest of her life. Not only that, her love affair with Paul Langevin was at an end.

THE STORMS OF WAR

In 1914, the First World War broke out and France was at war with Germany. (Of course, at the time, no one knew that there would be a *Second* World War, so they called it the Great War.) The Germans already occupied Poland, Marie's homeland, and she was deeply worried. She gave many donations to Polish causes but wanted to play a fully active part in the war effort.

ROVING RADIOLOGISTS

Since they'd been discovered in 1895, X-rays were beginning to be put to good use. People were starting to realize what an important tool they'd be for detecting broken bones. X-ray machines had been built and placed in hospitals to be used by radiologists. Radioactivity and radiology were closely connected and Marie knew how to make X-rays. This would be how she could help in the war. She set up radiology units to take X-ray photos of injured French soldiers, and she even helped build eighteen 'radiology cars'. These reached the more out-of-the-way places and, by the end of the war in 1918, these vehicles had helped examine over 10,000 wounded! Dressed in ordinary clothes, but wearing a red cross armband, Marie acted as radiologist, X-ray machine repairer and radiologist trainer. It was largely thanks to her, and those who worked with her, that the medical profession came to realize the true importance of X-rays.

TO AMERICA!

Less than three years later – based on some early suggestions for the possible uses of radium – an American supporter of Marie (who became a fund-raiser for her, raising over $100,000) promoted the idea that Marie's work on radioactivity was likely to lead to a cure for cancer. Marie herself believed that radium therapy might prove to have major medical benefits one day, but made no such wild claims. When Marie arrived in the US, with Irène and Eve, in May 1921, she was met by huge crowds in New York harbour. The highlight of the tour was at Carnegie Hall, with an audience of 35,000 women college students. Two days later, she even met the president. (Marie was to pay a second visit to the United States in 1929, and meet another president, but she was ill and that was to be a much more low-key, less happy experience.)

THE WORK GOES ON

Marie worked on tirelessly in many different areas for the rest of her life. She was involved in the creation of the Institute of Radium, and carried on her work at the Sorbonne, encouraging and training a new generation of scientists. She helped organize the system of publishing scientific papers and patenting ideas through her work for the League of Nations' Commission on Intellectual Co-operation. The 1920s and 30s was the period when people began to realize just what a terrible effect there was when working with radiation. Scientists – many of them Marie's friends and colleagues – were now dying of radiation poisoning. These new elements were dangerous. Marie herself was often in pain and always unwell now, but didn't talk about it. What mattered to her most was still her work.

A FAMILY WEDDING

On 9 October 1926, Marie's elder daughter, Irène, married the scientist Frédéric Joliot and she became Irène Joliot-Curie so as to keep the Curie name. They had three children. They called the youngest one Pierre. Marie was

deeply moved. Her husband's name lived on within the family. Like her parents before her, Irène worked with *her* husband on radioactivity – and this was to be work that was to eventually win them *their* Nobel Prize in 1935.

THE END COMES

Irène's mother didn't live to see them win it. After years of sickness, Marie Curie died of a form of leukaemia on 4 July 1934, aged 66. Two days later, she was buried in the cemetery at Sceaux, her coffin lowered on top of Pierre's. It was a small ceremony attended by family and close friends, including the Perrins and Paul Langevin. Sadly, Pierre's brother Jacques was too ill to attend and, off on holiday, Marie's sister Helena could not be reached with the news in time. Tributes, however, flooded in from around the world. They included a wreath from the president of Marie's beloved Poland. That was an honour of which she'd most certainly have been proud.

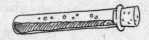

RADIATION AND CANCER

Although radiation can't actually cure cancer, today it IS used to treat some forms of the disease. Our bodies are made up of cells. Some types of cancerous cells are more sensitive to radiation than healthy cells. These can be killed without injuring the healthy ones, if the direction and amount of radiation is very carefully controlled. Many cancer patients' lives have been saved in this way. It's sad to think that the same radioactivity finally killed the woman who made it all possible.

TIMELINE
at home and abroad

1867	Marie Curie is born Marja Sklodowska
1874	Marie's sister Zofia dies of typhus
1878	Marie's mother dies
1887	*First Sherlock Holmes story is published*
1891	Marie goes to Paris
1894	Marie meets Pierre Curie for the first time
1895	Marie and Pierre marry
	Roentgen discovers X-rays
1896	Becquerel discovers uranium compounds give off rays too
1897	Daughter Irène is born
1898	The Curies discover new elements polonium and radium
1899	Ernest Rutherford publishes work on alpha and beta rays
1900	*Flight of the first Zeppelin airship*
	Paris's metro (underground railway) opens
1903	Marie, Pierre and Becquerel win Nobel Prize for Physics
1904	Marie and Pierre's daughter Eve is born
1906	Pierre killed in accident
1911	Marie wins Nobel Prize for Chemistry
1914	*Outbreak of First World War*
1918	*War ends*
1921	Marie's first trip to the US
1926	Irène marries

1933   *King Kong the movie is released*
1934   Marie Curie dies